RUN FASTER,
JUMP HIGHER,
THROW FARTHER

RUN FASTER, JUMP HIGHER, THROW FARTHER

How to Win at Track and Field

Louis Sabin

David McKay Company, Inc.

New York

Photos by Francene and Louis Sabin

Library of Congress Cataloging in Publication Data

Sabin, Louis.
   Run faster, jump higher, throw farther.

   Includes index.
   SUMMARY: A training guide for running, jumping, and
throwing.
   1. Track—athletics—Juvenile literature. 2. Track
—athletics—Training—Juvenile literature. [1. Track
and field]   I. Sabin, Francene.   II. Title.
GV1060.5.S22   796.4'2   79-3422
ISBN 0-679-20926-3

                    2 3 4 5 6 7 8 9 10
Manufactured in the United States of America

For Annie Bananie and Eddie Turquais

Contents

Introduction   ix

Running Events   1

1.	Sprinting	3
2.	Relay Passing	15
3.	Hurdles Races	21
4.	Distance Races	31
5.	Warming-Up Exercises	43

Jumping Events   49

6.	High Jumping	51
7.	Long Jumping	59
8.	Triple Jumping	65
9.	Pole Vaulting	73

Throwing Events   83

10.	Shot Putting	85
11.	Discus Throwing	93
12.	Javelin Throwing	103

Index   111

Introduction

Young athletes, no matter which sports they enjoy watching or playing, are almost always attracted to track and field. That's because the basic acts of running, throwing, and jumping are things most of us do naturally. And whether boys or girls play tennis, baseball, basketball, soccer, or football, they have to be able to run well to play well. Even if the sport is one that does not require players to run, the participants who are physically fit (because of many hours devoted to running) will be in fine shape to take part. This is true if the sport is golf, bowling, rowing, or any other physical activity that does not require you to run fast or a long distance. Staying power, or stamina, pays off in all sporting activities.

"What kind of runner am I?" That's a question many beginning runners ask themselves. Maybe they are not fast enough for sprint competition, but it is possible that they can run long distances and compete with pleasure in the mile or even the marathon.

There are a number of ways to find out whether you are best fitted for long or short distances in track competition. One way is to challenge others your age to friendly races. If you find you are beating just about everybody in short dashes, it's a good sign you may be a sprinter. If you don't do too well in those short races, try taking on others over longer distances. If you do well, then it's a good sign that you're a middle- or long-distance runner.

Another way to get an indication of where you will enjoy yourself most in the world of track is to run "against the clock." Wear a watch or ask a friend to time you while you run. Of course, the watch should have a second hand. The best timepiece to use is a stopwatch, which will allow you to measure your performance to the tenth of a second. This is especially important in timing sprint events.

It's possible you'll find that your times, in both the short and long distances, are not on a par with other runners, but don't give up hope. Your strengths may be in one or more of the field events. You could very well have the spring in your legs and strength in your shoulders to carry you way up in the high jump or pole vault, or far through the air in the long jump or triple jump.

Perhaps the muscle events — shot put, javelin, and discus — are the ones for you. You might even be blessed with the all-around abilities that qualify you for the decathlon — the event that tests an athlete's skills and endurance in ten track and field events. While it certainly would be glamorous to be known as the "World's Fastest Human" because you were the world's top sprinter, it would be equally glamorous to be known as the "World's Greatest Athlete" because you were the No. 1 decathlete on earth!

A fact of track that young athletes don't always understand is that, as you grow older, you may become better at an event in which you were not so good before. You might, for instance, lose a little speed but gain a lot of stamina. And suddenly, to your surprise, you'll stop competing in the

100-yard dash and start winning races at 880 yards or 1500 meters. This points up one of the truly wonderful things about the world of track and field. There are so many different events, each one requiring different talents, that just about any healthy boy or girl can find a place in the sport.

In the following pages, you will read about almost all the events engaged in by track and field athletes. Remember that these words of advice are written for a general audience, and that certain advice may not apply directly to you. For example, your coach might say, "I know the book says it is advisable to run five miles every morning. But I think you would profit by running an extra two miles a day." Don't argue the point. Your coach usually knows your physical and mental qualities very well, so let him or her be the judge of what's right and wrong for you.

One last word before we step onto the track. Running is something you will be able to do during your entire life. Unlike baseball, football, and many other team sports, running is not limited to any specific age group, nor does it require a special field or other players. That's why any runner — long after his or her days of organized competition are over, or even if he or she never made a track squad — will enjoy a healthier, happier life merely by continuing to run a while every day and by following the training and eating disciplines developed while still a young athlete.

RUNNING
EVENTS

1

Sprinting

Sprint races take place indoors and outdoors, and sprint events range from 50 yards and 50 meters to 440 yards and 400 meters. Because a sprint does not require as much strategy as longer races, it can be studied in very simple terms: 1) the start, 2) the dash, 3) the finish.

A fast, smooth start is critical for sprinting success, whether the race is 50 yards or 400 meters. For that reason, sprinters spend a great deal of time and effort practicing starts. The faster and stronger your getaway, the bigger your advantage will be over the not-so-well-prepared contestants in your races. A fast jump will often give you a lead of one or more yards right from the beginning. And that's a really big edge in a short race. Not only does it give you the actual edge in distance, it also gives you a mental edge: Your opponents *know* they are trailing right at the start!

Sprinters take their marks for a race with their feet set in starting blocks or in toeholes dug into the ground. Whether you start from blocks or holes, your feet should be in a position that will make them comfortable, not tense. However, that does not mean they should be so relaxed that they won't be ready to drive you forward when the starter signals the beginning of the race.

Set the first block (or dig the first hole) about 15 to 18 inches behind the starting line. The second block (or hole) should be 15 to 18 inches behind the first. (The back block is for your stronger foot, the one you normally use to kick a football or soccer ball.) You can use a ruler, or you can judge the distance by eye after you get into the "On your marks!" position. When you are in this position, the knee of your back foot should be on a line with the toes of your front foot. And don't forget the rule that both feet (usually the toe part of each shoe) must be touching the track once a runner takes the "On your marks!" position.

As soon as you have decided where your feet will be placed, stand up. Move to the starting line and bend forward until your hands are on the track a couple of inches in front of the line. Next, reach back with your "kicking" foot until it makes contact with the rear block and that knee is resting on the track. This done, settle your front foot into its block, but with your knee raised several inches above the track.

When your feet are in place, move your hands until they are just behind the starting line. Each hand should be lined up with its shoulder or slightly to the outside of the shoulder line. At this point, your hands should be spread in a bridge position — the thumb of each hand pointing inward, the fingers pointing outward. The portion of each hand that extends between the thumb and forefinger will be off the ground. The fingers should be pressed lightly against the track, but not so firmly that they feel strained or too tense. Keep in mind that the "On your marks!" position is for good balance. It is meant to make you comfortably prepared, so take care to set your hands and feet in a way that will give you the sense of being both relaxed and ready.

If you are properly balanced, most of your weight will be resting on the back knee, both hands, and a little on the front foot. The moment you have achieved that balance, lean forward until your shoulders are slightly in front of the starting line, and keep your eyes directed about four to six feet down the track.

After "On your marks!" the starter's next command will be "Set!" You then raise your hips until they are just a bit higher than the level of your shoulders. This shifts most of your weight onto your front leg and both arms, which should be held in a straight (but not elbows-locked) position. At this time your feet should be pressing against the blocks in readiness for the shove-off that will propel you forward. All of your muscles are tense and ready, and you are thinking of nothing but the starter's commands. Your whole body is alert for the word or gun sound that will send you flying down the track. Pay no attention to crowd noise or the runners near you.

"Go!" is signaled by the starter. You react instantly, surging from the blocks. At the same time, your arms come up, pumping in a back-and-forth motion. As one arm is driving forward and up, the other is driving back and down. The harder you pump your arms, the harder your legs will pump and carry your body forward.

Get into a long stride as soon as possible. Choppy running may give the feeling of speed, but it isn't as productive as long, smooth, powerful strides. Also, choppy running forces you to take more steps, and this places a greater demand on your arms, legs, and body. In brief, choppy running wastes precious energy.

As you drive forward from the blocks, arms pumping, lift each knee as high as you can. This action, combined with

The three steps to starting. First, get settled in the starting blocks. You want to be comfortable, not tense, before Step 2 — "On your marks!" Step 3 is the "set" position. You are alert for the start.

the reaching-forward thrust of your legs and your forward momentum, will give greater distance to your first steps and shift you into that power stride right away. So, if you were well balanced to begin with and are doing everything right, you will be charging ahead in a straight, even line, making it all the easier for you to get into that ground-eating stride.

"There are three things I remind myself before a race," says Steve Williams, the great American sprinter who set world records in the 100-yard, 100-meter, and 200-meter sprints, "and then *do* during the race. First, I tell myself, 'Back-block pressure!' to remind myself to push hard when the gun goes off. Second, I tell myself, 'Drive the left arm forward, like you're punching somebody with an uppercut!' to get my arms and legs into action instantly. And three, I tell myself, 'Accelerate!' when the times come to really turn it on in different parts of the race."

One of the worst enemies of the sprinter — or any athlete — is muscular tension. A fine line separates muscular tension from comfortable readiness, but you will learn how to achieve comfortable readiness through practice and with the aid of a coach or other experienced person. If no coach is around, have a friend or teammate watch you go through the starting positions and running down the track. If your friend sees that your arm swing is tight and jerky, or that your neck and shoulder muscles are as rigid as a board, you are too tense. And if, when you are running, your observer says that your face looks as if you are in great pain, and that your neck veins are standing way out, you still have the tension problem.

How can you know when your problems are fading or gone entirely? When your face shows no hint of pain or strain, and your body is in high gear while looking as if it's sailing along with no strain.

In any of the short sprints, from 50 yards through 100 meters, it is not possible to pace yourself. Any short sprint needs an all-out effort from start to finish. Even so, a sprinter normally takes 50 to 60 yards to reach full speed. That means, in a 100-yard dash, a sprinter is moving at top speed for 20 or 25 yards, until the muscles start to weaken at about the 80-yard mark. Now, a sprinter naturally loses speed because of tired leg muscles. At this point the sprinter must do two things. One, avoid "tying up" — getting so tense and tight that the body won't work at full efficiency. And two, keep good running form by holding a steady rhythm *and* pumping the arms hard to keep the knees lifting and the legs driving forward. Again, the key to success is lots of practice and mental preparation.

Finally, as you drive toward the tape, don't let up. Hold a strong, steady stride, keeping your eyes on the tape or even a spot a few feet beyond it. That way you will run right through the finish line. If it feels right to you to run right through the tape in a straight-up position, that's fine. Or if you want to lean into the finish a step or two from the tape, that's fine, too. Just do whatever feels most natural for you and produces the best results. Be sure, however, to decide what you are going to do *before* the race begins — and stay with that decision. A change of mind in the middle or at the end of the race can cause all kinds of problems for you, and could even cost you the race.

A wise runner should never make the mistake of being 100 percent sure the race is won until he or she is first across the finish line. But it does happen, even to champions like

Steve Williams. "I paid the price for being too sure too soon," Steve says. "I was in a 100-meter race against some top dash men, including Silvio Leonard of Cuba. I got away fast and built a good lead. I was sure I had it won. So I made the goof of letting down mentally, and began to kind of cruise into the finish line. I was sure that trophy was mine. Then here comes Leonard, bursting by on my left and leaning into the tape. He was first, not me, and I wanted to kick myself all the way around that track."

The 220-yard and 200-meter sprinters use the same starts, general form and driving finish as they do in shorter sprints. There is, however, an extra factor in running a successful 200 or 220. That is, during the course of this longer sprint, the runner must "float." This means that, for about 100 yards in the middle of the race, the runner goes as fast as possible *without reaching for that extra effort* saved for the last 50 or 60 yards. *Relaxed drive* are the words used to describe the midrace float. Just make sure you don't relax too much!

To sum it up, the pace for a 220-yard sprint would be: 1) an explosive start and driving pace for about 60 yards, 2) the "float" for about 100 yards, and 3) the all-out drive for the tape over the final 60 yards. Of course, if you are running in qualifying heats and want to save yourself for the finals, float for a longer distance, or don't drive all out for the tape. Just remember not to fail to qualify by letting up too much!

The longest sprints are the 440-yard and 400-meter events. These races also call for the same explosive start and driving finish as the shorter sprints. But in this case the float is a longer one, lasting from 120 to 150 yards in the middle of the race. This means that you are expected to sprint all out for much of the race, with the float coming in between the opening and closing sprints.

Clearly, then, these quarter-mile sprints call for real speed and endurance. To excel at this distance means that a runner must have more than the natural ability to run fast. It means that a runner must learn how to pace him or herself over the distance, and how to lean into the inside of the track while running the curve. So, you can see that a lot of training and discipline are "musts" for any runner with dreams of being a winner in a 400-meter or 440-yard race. But as every real athlete knows, that's true of every event in track and field.

"Here's how I look at the basic approaches to the three sprints," says Steve Williams. "In the 100 there is no pace. You just get out of the blocks as fast as you can and *keep on, keep on, keep on* till the race is over.

"There *is* a pace for the 220. You try to run as fast as you can, but also as relaxed and efficiently as possible. Getting the feel of the float is very important.

"What many athletes do wrong in running the sprints is thinking they have to run fast and tense. This causes them to fail to relax. When you're running tense your muscles tighten like wires and you can't reach out as far as you should. I always think of a tense runner being like a machine without any oil — the parts work with too much effort!

"Relaxing is just as important in the 440," Steve explains. "It's just a longer period of running relaxed and fast in the middle of the race. Another thing about the 440: a runner has to learn to take the curve as well balanced as possible, while also being as relaxed and as quick as possible. This keeps you flowing around the bend, and that momentum is still there as you come out of the bend and head for home. But if you don't run relaxed, you're going to tie up after you come out of the curve, and lose the race."

What follows is a general schedule for training as a sprinter. You, or your coach, may want to alter it. What matters most is that you follow a regular program of practice — working at it from 30 to 60 minutes every day, five days a week.

Off-Season Training Schedule

Monday, Wednesday, Friday:

1. Run three miles at an even, easy pace.
2. Using blocks, do five 60-yard sprints, each time jogging around the track back to the blocks.
3. Do four 100-yard sprints from the blocks, jogging around the track after the last one.
4. Do four 220-yard sprints, using blocks, and finish up by jogging twice around the track.

All starts should follow what you read about "On your marks!" "Set!" and "Go!" The sprints should be run as seriously as if you were in a race. Conditioning is mental as well as physical.

Tuesday, Thursday:

1. Run three miles at an even, easy pace.
2. Do ten 150-yard sprints, all-out, walking back to the blocks after each of the first nine, and jogging around the track back to the blocks after the last one.

3. Do one 100-yard, one 200-yard, then one 300-yard sprint, returning to the blocks each time. Repeat this series three times.

Regular-Season Training Schedule

Monday through Friday:

1. Begin each day's schedule with an even, easy-paced mile run, followed by a five-minute rest.
2. Do four 120-yard sprints, using blocks.
3. Rest for two minutes. Do four 75-yard sprints, using blocks.
4. Rest for two minutes. Do four 200-yard sprints.
5. Rest for three minutes. Do three 50-yard sprints.

If your coach has you on a weight-training program, finish the day's workout with that. If not, run a series of four brisk quarter miles. On weekend days, when there is no meet, keep up your muscle tone by doing some sort of exercise — jogging, bicycle riding, swimming laps.

Note: If your training program is not being supervised, be your own watchdog. That means do not put too much strain on your muscles, and do not work beyond your capacity. If you find you are very tired the day after a workout, you are probably overdoing it. Cut down on the demands you are making of yourself. You will soon be able to judge just how much is right for you.

2
Relay Passing

Track and field events are not in the category of team sports. Yet one part of this sport does require grade-A teamwork: the relay. There are a number of different sprint relay races: the 4 x 110-yard relay (four runners, each sprinting 110 yards), the 4 x 220 (four runners, each sprinting 220 yards), and the 4 x 440 (four runners, each sprinting 440 yards).

There are also distance relays, with each of the four runners going longer distances than in the sprint relays.

Finally, there are medley relays, in which four runners race varying distances. One example of this last group is the sprint medley, which calls for the four contestants to run distances in this order: 440 yards, 220 yards, 220 yards, and 880 yards.

Speed and stamina are necessary for success in any relay race. But there is something else of equal, if not greater, importance. That is for a relay team to be able to pass the baton, or stick, swiftly *and* well. The pass, also called the exchange, takes place three times during a relay race. The first runner passes to the second, who passes to the third, who passes to the fourth.

Each pass is done in a passing zone, which is 20 meters long. This means, for example, that runner No. 1 in the sprint medley (440, 220, 220, 880) must pass the baton to runner No. 2 within that 20-meter section of the track, after finishing the 440-yard run.

Runner No. 2 then sprints 220 yards and reaches the next passing zone, where the baton must be passed to runner No. 3 within another 20-meter zone. This is repeated one more time, when runner No. 3 passes the baton to runner No. 4.

The baton is exchanged in one of two forms of passing — open or closed. The *open* pass, used in distance relays, is done this way: Runner A, who is to get the baton from runner B, looks over his or her right shoulder at the incoming teammate. When runner B is getting close to the passing zone, runner A starts to run forward, keeping eyes on the baton, at the same time extending the right hand backward, palm up. And keeping it there until runner B slaps the baton down into the open palm. (A second way for runner A to take the baton is also with the palm of the right hand extended straight back. Then runner B will slap the baton between runner A's thumb and forefinger.)

The *closed* pass, favored for use in sprint relays, is done this way: Runner B, who is to take the pass, does not watch the incoming runner A when the pass is made. Instead, runner B starts to run the second leg of the race, at the same time extending the right hand backward to get the baton. Runner A will slap the baton into runner B's palm in one of three ways:

1. As the baton comes down, runner B's palm faces up, the hand turned so that the elbow faces down and the thumb points at runner A;

The open pass.

The closed pass.

2. As the baton comes down, B's palm faces up, the hand turned so that the elbow faces up and the thumb points to the left;

3. The baton is slapped up into the "V" made by runner B's thumb and forefinger. For this pass, runner B's right arm is almost straight and trailing slightly toward the rear.

Each of the passes must be done with precise timing on the parts of both the passer and the receiver. This can come about only through repeated practice sessions. And while both must play the role well in the exchange, it should be kept in mind that the passer carries the greater responsibility. That is because the passer has the action in front and can see where the teammate's hand is, if anything is wrong in the passing zone, and so forth.

It is also up to the passer to make sure to slap the baton firmly into the teammate's hand and keep it there *just long enough* for the teammate to have full control of it. If the passer lets go of the baton too soon, it can fall to the ground. If the passer lets go of it too late, it will force the teammate to twist the body, break stride, and lose precious yards.

So, it should not surprise you to learn that a smooth-passing relay team can often beat a team that is faster but does not pass as well. Fractions of seconds count, whether they are gained (or lost) by swift-moving feet or hands. As you can see, there is more to the relay than plain speed and stamina!

3

Hurdles Races

When it is done just right, hurdling is one of the most beautiful athletic sights in the world. The runner sprints from the blocks toward the first hurdle, nears it, whips the lead leg up and over, and folds the upper body in a forceful, graceful bow. Even as the lead leg skims the hurdle, and the opposite hand stretches toward the foot of the lead leg, the trailing leg is coming up — bending out like a wing over the hurdle bar.

Now the hurdler's hips twist with the smoothness of a well-oiled machine. The lead leg drops toward the track. The trailing leg snaps past the hurdle and down. It is as if the athlete is trying to make the trailing leg do something impossible — reach the ground *before* the lead leg.

And, without a break in the fluid forward motion, the hurdler sprints toward the next hurdle. Again the lead leg lifts, the opposite hand stretches toward the foot of the lead leg, and so on.

As this description shows, hurdlers must do two things well: 1) run with a sprinter's speed, and 2) control their bodies while dashing between and over the hurdles. So, first of all, good hurdlers must have the qualities of good sprinters. That means they must practice starts and sprinting technique. On top of that, they must learn to control their strides in order to take the same number of strides from one hurdle to the next. And finally, they must learn and master the *raise, kick,* and *snap* of getting over each hurdle.

Not counting the shorter, indoor races, there are five hurdle events: 1) 120-yard high hurdles; 2) 110-meter hurdles, 3) 180-yard low hurdles, 4) 440-yard intermediate hurdles, and 5) 400-meter intermediate hurdles. For young, developing runners, the 110-meter hurdles race is the one most coaches recommend. That is because it is a shorter distance, requiring less stamina, and because the hurdles are not too high. Low hurdles are 30 inches from the ground, while high hurdles stand as much as 39 inches high.

If you are not on a track team or cannot practice on a school track, try to borrow hurdles from the local recreation department. You also can ask local school or recreation authorities if they have any old hurdles to spare. You can fix them up. You will need at least three hurdles. Set the first one 15 yards down the track from the starting line. Set all the others 10 yards apart.

Using a sprinter's start, explode out of the starting block and approach the first hurdle. Keep your eyes trained on the top of the hurdle. When it is time to clear that first hurdle, raise your lead leg high and start to straighten it. At the same moment, give yourself thrust and height by pushing off and up on the toes of your trailing foot. This action is called the *raise.*

Your aim is to have the lead foot clear the hurdle as close as possible without hitting it. (You want to get over the hurdle and back to the ground as fast as you can. But you also don't want to hit the barrier, which could force you to break form, even stumble and fall.) Straighten the lead leg until the knee is almost locked. As this is being done, bend your body forward from the waist as if you want your chin to touch your knee. Reach your opposite hand either straight ahead, or toward the front of your lead foot. The other arm either reaches for that same lead foot, or is extended to the side for balance. This action is called the *kick*.

The third move is to *snap* the lead foot back down to the track. Do this as quickly as you can. You want to be running on the ground as much as possible, and in the air as short a time as possible. That's because you move a lot faster while running than while floating in air.

Even as you are snapping that lead foot down, you are pulling the trailing foot over the hurdle. (This is one of the crucial moves for the hurdler, so study it well and practice it repeatedly.) The hips are turning so that your lead leg will be able to swing up and out. This action is almost like a bird raising and bending its wing as it swoops close to a wave.

Now, as your lead knee just clears the hurdle, make sure your shoulders are square ahead and you are facing straight down the track. You want to maintain good balance. Also, take special care to turn your lead foot up, so that the shoe will not clip the hurdle at the last instant.

Your lead foot snaps to the track. Your trailing foot skims past the bar. Your body comes out of the forward bend, bringing you back into sprinting position. If your shoulders stayed square ahead, your form held, and neither leg hit the hurdle, your eyes should see nothing but the next hurdle as you fly toward it.

One more thing: Remember to keep the knee of the trailing leg high all the way through the hurdling process. This will keep your stride long when you land, the way it has to

*The lead, or hurdle-clearing, foot may be either the right or left
foot. Remember to keep the knee of the trailing leg high.*

be if you don't want to lose time and distance between hurdles. Now, put it all together and you'll be ready to run a winning race!

What is in the mind of a world-class hurdler is described by Renaldo Nehemiah, record-setter at every hurdle distance from 50 yards to 110 meters. "I think about what I have to do to win that race. I don't think about setting records, or worry about the other guys in the race. I concentrate on getting a good start. Then I concentrate on each hurdle — clearing it cleanly, not hitting it. And then I think about the proper finish for that particular race. It's a combination of concentration, relaxation, and putting together all the things I work on in practice. With all that on my mind, I have no room to worry about anybody else in the race. Which is the way it should be.

"Once the race starts," Nehemiah explains, "I run as if the hurdles aren't even there, even though I know they are. I go at the race as if it's a sprint, with a giant step to take every time I get to a hurdle.

"I also do something no other hurdler does — talk to myself all through the race. That makes me fully aware of what I'm doing from start to finish. For instance, if I go over a hurdle right, I say, 'Good! Go to the next one.' But if I hit a hurdle, I say, 'Don't panic. Stay cool. You can't go back and make it up.' So, if I'm too high or too low over a hurdle, I tell myself to make the correction for the next one. I also tell myself, 'Lift your knees high.' And 'run harder, harder.' And 'don't let up till you're through the tape.' Maybe it's crazy, but it works for me!"

It is a good idea to practice different parts of hurdling in a standing position or by clearing an imaginary hurdle. And, as you go through the motions, say out loud each thing you do. Start slowly. Then, when you feel you have the move down pat, increase the speed of the exercise. In a way, it's like practicing scales on the piano. Start slowly, letting the body do what the brain tells it to, then playing the notes faster and faster as you get better and better.

Along with practicing the *raise, kick,* and *snap* motions, you should practice two other important parts of hurdling: 1) getting from the starting line to the first hurdle in the right position for takeoff, and 2) getting from one hurdle to the next so that you are in perfect takeoff position.

If you are getting to a hurdle too close or too far away for a perfect takeoff, you will have to take shorter or longer strides. There is only one way to find out what you are doing wrong and correct it: by actually doing it, again and again.

There are two things to keep in mind:

1) Make sure you take off on the same foot every time.

2) If you find you are having trouble learning while using the racing hurdles, make a change. For example, you can push a couple of sticks into the ground and stretch a string between them at the proper height. This will be the "hurdle," and you won't have to worry about falling or skinning yourself. Also, it's a big help to have someone watch you, to tell you what you are doing right and wrong.

You've probably heard it said a thousand times, but it's true — practice does make perfect. Every top athlete, like Renaldo Nehemiah, will tell you it's so. "I was never a natural at any sport, including track," the great hurdler says. "I had to work hard to become a good basketball player, a good football player, and a winner on the track. That's why I tell every young athlete to stick with what he or she is doing, to work harder whether you're doing well or not so good. That's the only way to succeed at any sport."

"But I have to add something to that. Which is: There's time enough to have fun before you get really serious about sports. Wait until you're in your teens to start getting serious. When you're young, you should just have fun, enjoy whatever you're doing.

"Also, don't get pegged in one event — you may be even better in a different one. Like, I was told I was a quarter-miler when I was in high school. But, as I found out by trying other track and field events, I was best suited for the hurdles. A good coach will let you find your own event, and then help you do your best at whichever one you choose. I believe nobody is going to do really well if he doesn't honestly enjoy what he's doing."

Training sessions for hurdlers come in two separate but related sections. One section follows the schedule for sprinters' workouts. This includes the easy-distance runs for endurance, the starts, the dashes, etc. The other section is for actual hurdling — stride and pace between hurdles, clearing the hurdles, etc.

Off-Season Training Schedule

Monday:

1. Run three miles at an even, easy pace.
2. Using blocks, do five 60-yard sprints, each time jogging back to the blocks.
3. Do four 100-yard sprints from the blocks, jogging back each time.
4. Do three 220-yard sprints, using blocks, and finish up by jogging twice around the track.

Tuesday:

1. Using blocks and sprint starts, clear three hurdles in racing form. Repeat five times.
2. Do wind-sprints around the track, 120 yards each, with a brief recovery jog between each sprint.
3. Repeat No. 1, three times.
4. Work on problems, i.e. pacing, form over hurdles, etc.

Wednesday:

1. Run three miles at an even, easy pace.
2. Do four 120-yard sprints from the blocks.
3. Do four 440-yard sprints, all out, with a two-minute walk in between each.
4. Work to eliminate problems.

Thursday:

Repeat Monday.

Friday:

Repeat Tuesday.

Regular-Season Training Schedule

Monday:

1. Using blocks and three hurdles, do five sprint starts and all-out running. Jog back after each.
2. Repeat No. 1, continuing after last hurdle until 120 yards are covered on each sprint.
3. Practice weight training (if recommended by coach).

Tuesday:

1. Using blocks and six hurdles, sprint-start and all-out run for 120 yards. Rest two minutes. Repeat.
2. Run 120-yard sprints without hurdles.
3. Using blocks and three hurdles, do two sprint starts followed by all-out running, with 30-second rest in between.
4. Lift weights or work to correct problems.

Wednesday:

1. Using blocks, do three sprint starts and clear first hurdle.
2. Run two 120-yard sprints without hurdles, jogging back to blocks.
3. Practice three sprint starts from blocks and medium-paced run over eight hurdles. Jog back to blocks.
4. Run four 50-yard sprints from blocks, concentrating on fast start.

Thursday:

1. Using blocks, do three sprint starts and clear three hurdles each time.
2. Using blocks, run four 100-yard sprints, jogging back.
3. Run four 75-yard sprints, with a 15-second breather after each.

Friday:

No actual running if meet is scheduled for Saturday. Just do loosening-up exercises and standing-in-place, hurdle-clearing motions. If a meet is scheduled for a weekday, follow the Friday schedule the day before the meet.

4

Distance Races

There are people who think the sprints are the most important events in track and field. They point out that the 100-meter champion is famous as "the world's fastest human." That is true, of course. But they seem to forget such equally famous runners as Roger Bannister, Jim Ryun, Frank Shorter, and Lasse Viren. Bannister and Ryun were great middle-distance runners, while Shorter and Viren were champions in long-distance events.

One of these all-time champions makes a special point about his kind of running. "One of the best things about distance running," says Frank Shorter, America's gold-medal winner in the marathon at the 1972 Olympics, "is that it is never boring. You can think about all kinds of things. You can train by yourself or with others. And the fact is, distance runners like to get away from everyday life. There's nothing more peaceful than being out by yourself, loping through the woods, where it's really beautiful. What makes distance runners different from all other athletes is that they like their training even more than actually racing. It also gives us a special feeling about ourselves — of being healthy, in fine condition, and knowing we can continue to run for years and years and years."

So, even if you aren't as fast as a lot of other runners, don't give up hope of finding a place for yourself in track. And don't stop dreaming of being a top track performer. You may not have great speed, but you may be blessed with great endurance.

You could be physically right to run the middle-distance events: 880 yards, 800 meters, 1000 yards, 1500 meters, or the mile. Anything longer than a mile is usually called long-distance.

The 880. Building up endurance — to have the strength and staying power to run a long way with a fair amount of speed — takes plenty of work. You should plan to work at any middle-distance event for most of the year. But even if you take a break in the summer, you should be back in training when school starts again.

Preseason Training. At least once every week, run or jog no less than one mile, more if possible. And try to run one time on a track or hard path, another time up and down hills, and another time on grass or along the seashore. This is how you build your muscles and "wind."

After two or three weeks of this getting-back-in-shape work, start to do some harder running. Every weekday, run four 400-yard sprints. Don't go all out, but don't take it easy, either. After each sprint, walk the same distance. It's a good idea to wear a watch while you are training. This will help you to keep a record of the time it takes you to run each sprint. The time should be the same for each 400-yarder, or close to it.

At the end of the third week of this training, add two 100-yard sprints to the schedule. Do these after you take a 10-minute rest from the four 400-yard sprints.

Follow this schedule for two weeks. Then, once you are in

good condition, you will be ready to do six 400-yard sprints on Monday, Wednesday and Friday. Push yourself almost to the limit.

On Tuesday, do four 200-yard sprints, close to all-out. Walk 200 yards after each of the first three. After the last 220, take an easy run around the track, followed by a strong, but not all-out, 440-yard sprint. Finish up with a 200-yard walk, then sprint as hard as you can until you are exhausted.

On Thursday, run an easy mile. Rest for ten minutes, then do two medium-paced 440-yard runs. Rest five minutes. Do a medium-fast 880-yard run. Rest two minutes. Finish with a jog around the track.

At no time should you strain your body. If you feel "beat" the day after a workout, take a day off or just jog a little. While you will miss a training period, it is important to do so. You want to stay free of muscle pulls and injuries that come from putting too much stress on the body. Problems like that can keep you out of action for days — or even weeks — at a time.

In an 880 race, runners use the sprinter's start or a half-crouch start. Once the race begins, you have a choice of three basic ways to run the race: 1) in the lead, 2) in the pack, 3) in back of the others. Unless your coach tells you otherwise, the best place to be for most of the race is just behind the leader(s). Just make sure the pace for the first 440 yards isn't too fast. If it is, don't stay with it — you'll burn yourself out and have nothing left for the second half of the race.

Keep up a long, relaxed stride. After the first 440 yards, stay right with the leader or take the lead yourself. Whichever you do, remember that you want to be very strong over the last 220 yards. That's when your training will pay off. You'll turn back any challenge and outkick anyone who hasn't done the hard work to get ready for the *whole* race.

The Mile. Training for the mile or the 1500-meter run is a year-round job. And there is no better kind of training than cross-country running to build up endurance, and body and leg muscles. If you live in a basically cool climate, do this in late summer and in the fall until bitter cold weather forces you onto indoor tracks.

Even when you are not running — inside or outside — you must work to build strength in other ways. One is by bicycling. Another is through the use of weights, to develop legs, arms, and upper body. Swimming is another good way to stay in shape in a relaxed way. But when it comes to weight work, be sure to have the advice of a coach!

Training for the mile is a lot like training for the 880-yard or 1000-yard run. That is, you have to do a lot of 440-yard runs, plus some sprinting for speed, and some 880-yard runs for endurance, pacing, and stride.

Off-Season Training Schedule

Monday, Wednesday: Run cross-country or around a track. Jog 440 yards, then sprint 440 yards, then jog another 440 yards. Then sprint 220 yards and jog 220 yards. (If you are running cross-country, make a point to sprint up hills. Such training is not possible on a flat track, of course, which is why cross-country or sand running is recommended at least once a week.) Repeat this drill three times, unless too tired. Remember: Don't quit too quickly, but don't take a chance on injuring yourself, either.

Tuesday, Thursday: Work on building speed. Start with a

series of: 100-yard sprint, 100-yard walk, 220-yard sprint, two-minute rest. Do 440-yard sprint, 100-yard walk, 50-yard sprint. Take a seven-minute break, then repeat all the events in sequence.

All together, a day's running on Monday through Thursday should be close to four times the distance of the race you are training to run. So, for the mile, you should cover a total of four miles each day.

On Friday, Saturday or Sunday: Run around a track or cross-country for one nonstop mile. After the run, do a light workout with weights or calisthenics. Then, if possible, ride a bicycle for several miles. (Saturday or Sunday is your day off, depending on which one you devote to working out.)

Regular-Season Training schedule

Monday, Wednesday: Run one hour at a strong, steady pace. After a ten-minute rest, do a 440-yard run just below the all-out level. Jog for 440 yards, then do a 50-yard sprint, 50-yard walk, and a 100-yard sprint. After a five-minute rest, do an 880-yard run at a moderate pace.

Tuesday, Thursday: Do a short series: 50-yard jog, 50-yard sprint, 50-yard walk. Repeat four times, then take a five-minute rest. Do a 100-yard sprint, 100-yard walk, 50-yard sprint. Follow with weight training or calisthenics, as advised by your coach.

Friday, Saturday or Sunday: Run at a relaxed, steady rate for two hours.

When there is a race to be run, take a relaxed, one-hour jog the day before. As you run, review the strategy of the race. Get to bed early.

The mile and every race longer than a mile begins with a standing start. The five parts of the start follow the sequence below:

1) At the command, "Take your mark!" put one foot just behind the starting line,

2) Put the other foot in back of, and slightly to one side of, the first. Both feet (and the rest of you) should be relaxed,

3) If your left foot is at the line, your right arm should be bent at the elbow, as if you were running. Your left arm should be held loosely near your left hip,

4) At the command, "Set!" crouch forward slightly and bend your knees a bit,

5) At the command, "Go!" start moving away from the line quickly. Get into your distance stride as soon as possible.

At the start, don't get caught in the fight for position. The elbow and shoulder battles take too much wasted energy. Either get out in front on speed alone or settle into a position near the rear. World-class milers run anywhere from first to last place at the start. They judge according to how they feel that day or according to who else is in the race. It is more important to get into your distance-running stride and to set the pace that's right for you. Don't let others change your strategy. If that happens, you may find you are too far behind by the last 220 yards to make a run for the tape. Or you may not have enough energy left because you were tricked into running too fast too early in the race.

Long-distance Running: Anything beyond the mile is long-distance running. Training to run all distances from the two-mile race to the marathon (26 miles, 385 yards) depends on a lot of things. Each runner is different. Coaches

For the longer races, runners make a standing start. Notice how these runners all seem to be in perfect rhythm as their race begins.

have various ideas of how to train. Running surfaces and weather conditions differ. That is why it is best for each runner to speak with his or her coach about a training schedule, weight work, diet, and other factors.

It is true, however, that all distance runners must be ready to devote themselves to year-round training. Some time will be spent on a track, doing supervised sprint work. Even more time will be spent getting in shape by running long distances. Running cross-country through woods, up and down hills, over different kinds of surfaces — all build endurance and strength. And all prepare the runner for the drain on his or her oxygen supply. That drain is the toughest part of long-distance running.

Describing his training method for the marathon, Frank Shorter says, "When I'm running on the track, which I do three days a week, I run hard bursts with as little time as possible in between each burst. They will be at distances of 220, 440, 880, and 1320 yards. That's when I'm training at my maximum of effort. It is about 90 percent of the effort I give in an actual race.

"As I run in training I think about the times it takes me to cover each distance. I also think about ways to motivate myself for the upcoming race. One of the things I do is imagine the race taking place, and me pushing myself harder and harder to win.

"That on-track running I described is called 'interval training.' It's a very important part of a runner's schedule. The running you do on the other four days of the week is necessary. But it is not nearly as important as the quality and high intensity of those three hard days."

On the matter of weights, Shorter says: "I do a moderate amount of weight-lifting. I lift very light weights and do a

As the great Villanova middle-distance star, Don Paige, shows, good form means a long, relaxed stride until the final drive for the tape.

lot of repetitions. This is only to give my arms enough strength for the sprint at the end of the race. It's not a big muscle-building thing. When you run, the only part of your body you don't exercise is your arms. So, you don't want to let them get weak — you need them to keep pumping, driving your legs onward. The stronger your arms are, the faster you can move them. And the faster they go, the faster your legs will go.

"In running the marathon," Shorter continues, "you should not get too excited. If you do, you'll use up all your mental energy, something you really need as the race gets longer. A marathoner has to wait about 20 miles before he gets really serious about it. That's when you have used up most of your calories. Then a change comes over your body, and you have to work your way through that. It's the hardest part of the race.

"People have described that part as the painful part. But it's not pain. It's really fatigue, just being plain worn out. It's a kind of numbness, like your body is slipping away from you. So, at that moment I start to think of how far I've come and how little I have left to go. And I just keep going until I've crossed the finish line!"

Be sure to wear comfortable clothing, like a sweatsuit, when training. And be especially careful to wear the right kinds of socks and shoes. (Your coach or sporting goods sales clerk can advise you on these.) Also, *be certain to have a medical check-up before starting on any running program!*

If you plan to run in very hot or humid weather, take care not to suffer from heat exhaustion. Drink liquids along the way, and wet your body whenever possible. And if the weather is cold, protect your ears and hands from frostbite, by wearing gloves, headbands, earmuffs, etc.

On the matter of diet for distance runners, there are different opinions. The great American distance runner, Bill Rodgers, says that he eats anything he wants; but he makes sure he has plenty of carbohydrates in his diet. So does Frank Shorter, who says, "I don't eat anything special, and I eat only one big meal a day. Like all distance runners, I eat plenty of spaghetti and other foods rich in carbohydrates. I eat cereals in the morning, cakes and candies during the day. That's because carbohydrates supply the fuel a runner burns up. And I eat a big dinner after finishing up the day's training. I don't take any vitamin supplements, protein pills, or that kind of stuff. Food gives me just about everything I need, and I believe the natural sources are the best."

When it comes to distance running, Shorter, Rodgers, and all the other experts have one belief: Run and have fun. That, as much as anything, is what running is all about.

5
Warming-Up Exercises

You are going to run, or throw, or jump. But before you start, there is something you must remember to do — warm-up exercises. That's because you want the muscles in your legs, arms, and back to be loose. That way, you'll avoid muscle pulls and injuries. You also want to be warm, because a cold muscle is a tight muscle, and tight muscles are no good for track and field performers. In addition, you want to be physically relaxed because that will help you be mentally relaxed. In short, warming up is an important part of the athlete's getting-ready routine.

The following ten warm-up exercises are for use before a practice workout or an actual competition. Choose *at least* five different kinds to do before training or competing.

1. *Arm swinging.* Drop your shoulders as low as you can. Then, swing your arms up and down, as if you are running. Bend the elbows, relax the body, and breathe evenly. After a few seconds, pick up the speed of the swing gradually until you are pumping as fast as possible. Now stop, relax, and repeat the exercise two more times.

Here is a variation of the arm swing. Swing one arm easily, around and around, like a windmill. Keep the arm extended but not stiff, for about 30 seconds at a time, then swing the other arm. Exercise for five minutes.

2. *Running in place.* Staying in one place, run with proper form. That means: Lift your knees high and keep your back fairly straight, leaning forward just a little. To get full value from this exercise, stay on your toes as you run. Keep up a moderate pace, with the body relaxed.

3. *Bicycle ride.* While lying on your back, raise your legs and hips as high as you can. Keep your head, neck, and shoulders pressed against the ground. Then, with your hands placed just behind your hips, pump your legs in the air as if you were riding a bicycle. Remember, the purpose is only to loosen and warm your muscles, so relax and don't strain yourself.

4. *Leg kicking.* Standing in place, kick one leg into the air as high as you can. With each leg kick, raise both hands and gently catch the foot with them. Then lower the foot. Do 15 kicks with one foot, then 15 with the other. Rest one minute, then repeat.

5. *Sit and stretch.* Sit on the ground as if you were clearing a hurdle, with the right leg trailing. Stretch your right hand until it touches your left foot. At the same time, bend your head to your left knee. Do 15 stretches, then change position so that the left leg is trailing. Do 15 stretches. Rest one minute, then repeat.

6. *Leg raise and spread.* Lie on your back, with your arms and palms against the ground. Keep both legs stiff and lift them off the ground. Slowly spread them apart as far as they can go, then bring them together slowly. Lower your legs to the ground. Repeat this exercise ten times, with a five-second rest after each.

7. *Leg raise.* This is the same as exercise 6, but without the spread. Hold your legs in the air for ten seconds on each raise.

8. *Leg behind head.* Get into the *Bicycle ride* position

*Warm-up exercises before a workout or a race are very impor-
tant. If your muscles aren't loose and relaxed, you could sustain
an injury.*

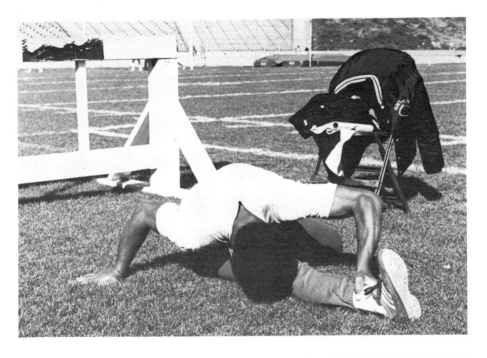

(exercise 3). Instead of pumping your legs, hold them steady. Then touch the ground behind your head with the toe of one foot. Return your legs to one lifted-together position, hold them steady, then touch the ground behind your head with the toe of the other foot. Repeat this four times. Rest two minutes. Repeat the entire exercise (five times for each foot).

9. *Bend and stretch.* Move your legs apart about three or four feet. Bend one knee, then lean sideways until the full weight of your body is on the leg of the bent knee. At the same time, stretch the other leg to the side in a stiff position. Reverse the exercise to stretch your other leg. Repeat this exercise ten times for each leg. Take care not to strain the muscles of the stiff leg or to lose your balance.

10. *Toe touchers.* Stand with your legs about two feet apart. Raise your hands straight above your head, reach down and touch both feet at the same time. Keeping your body relaxed and breathing easily, do 20 touches, raising your arms above your head between each one. One variation of this exercise is to hold your hands together above your head (shake hands with yourself), then bring them down to the left foot, raise them above your head, and bring them down to the right foot. Also do 20 touches. A third variation is to bring your hands straight down to the ground, touching it with your knuckles or palms. Also do 20 touches.

Your coach may have some other warming-up exercises he or she favors. That's fine, as long as you do them regularly and correctly. Remember: A well-tuned body can avoid strains and pulls if it has had the chance to loosen and warm up before the athlete starts to practice or compete.

JUMPING EVENTS

6
High Jumping

There are two basic styles of high jumping: the straddle and the flop. In doing the straddle, the jumper passes over the crossbar facing the ground. In doing the flop, the jumper clears the crossbar facing the sky. However, no matter which style of jump you like, never jump without mats, a foam-rubber pad, or thick layers of sawdust or wood shavings to land on. You run a high risk of injury if you don't land on a surface that is soft enough.

All high jumpers must run to the crossbar with a *fast but controlled* approach. The number of steps you take from start to jump may be anywhere from eight to twelve. The side you approach from is also up to you. And, like hurdlers, high jumpers have to find out which leg is their "take-off" leg. A few tries on each leg and a few trial runs will tell you which one is right for you.

The Straddle. Let's say you are going to 1) take off on your left leg, 2) use an eleven-step approach, and 3) start from a spot about 50 feet from and to the left side of the high-jump pit. Relax. Think about what you are going to do. Ready? Start your approach with a strong push-stride off your left foot onto your right foot. This is step 1. Now, keep on going, using the next four steps to gather *controlled speed.* The final six steps, at that good pace, will carry you to the crossbar, and up.

Some jumpers come at the bar in a direct line. Others take a gently curving route in the last six steps. There are other approaches, but most of the top jumpers like the curving route. In any case, remember that the last three steps are the key to a successful jump. They give you the big lift!

On step nine, start to lean back, letting your lead foot get ahead of your body. This step is longer than the ones you took before. And the next two are even longer. As you take these two steps, your arms move with a motion that brings the elbows curving in toward your sides and then up. (This arm thrust is a gathering of strength for the explosive double-arm lift. It will combine with your lead leg to launch your leap.) As you take these last three steps, continue to lean back farther.

Now, as the heel of your take-off foot hits the ground, drive both arms and the lead knee up. Don't aim for the crossbar. Aim for a point in front of the crossbar and higher than the crossbar. Your speed and thrust will carry you forward and over the crossbar.

You are now into the power push of the high jump. Your lead leg — either bent at the knee or straight — is the first part of your body over the crossbar. Keep the rest of your body straight. As the lead leg clears the crossbar, the body begins its roll over the crossbar. (Imagine you are turning inside a rotating barrel.) At this point, your body should be in a parallel line with the crossbar.

As the body rolls over the crossbar, your left arm and hand are tucked either against your chest or above and behind your left hip. The right arm is straight and the hand is pointing in the direction of the jump, to help carry you over. Kick the trailing leg straight out and up. That way, it

The straddle.

will not hit the crossbar as you finish the roll and drop into the pit.

If you hit the crossbar on the way up, your take-off point was too close. So try again, taking off a bit farther away from the crossbar. But if you came down on the crossbar or even in front of it, then your take-off point was too far away. So move your take-off point a little closer and try again.

The Flop. Again, we will assume an eleven-step approach and a take-off from the left foot. However, you are going to start about 50 feet back and to the *right* of the high-jump pit. All the directions for the first eight steps of the straddle are the same as for the flop — the fast approach, the curving route, the lean-back, the gathering of arms for the explosive lift-off, the bent lead knee thrusting you up. But at step 9 you change direction as you reach the point where you start to raise your arms for the lift-off.

You cut from the right side toward the middle of the crossbar, turning your body so that, when your left leg hits the ground for takeoff, your right elbow will be pointing at the pit. As you leave the ground, your back is toward the crossbar. By the time you are nearing the peak of your jump: 1) your arms will be close to your sides, 2) your legs will begin to fold like a frog's (knees apart wide, feet touching), and 3) your head and shoulders will be passing over the crossbar.

As your head begins to bend backwards toward the pit, you are helping the rest of your body to clear the crossbar. Do this by lifting your knees and feet. This will raise your hips past the crossbar. Next, lift your arms. This action will lift your feet, snapping them over the crossbar. Once your feet are over, relax for a landing that will bring your shoulders, neck, and head to the soft pad below.

It is a good idea for beginners to practice with the cross-

The Flop.

*The jumper doing the Flop is the remarkable Franklin Jacobs,
whose powerful takeoff and graceful form enabled him to leap
almost two feet over his own height of 5'8'' — a world record!
(Dan Murphy)*

bar set at a height of 2½ feet. What matters most is that you develop the right technique. Once you do, success will follow. No training schedule is given. All high jumpers train by jumping. They otherwise stay in good physical condition by running laps for endurance, sprinting to develop speed and strength, and maintain sensible eating and sleeping habits.

The right technique and great determination made America's Franklin Jacobs a champion high jumper. "My jump looks like the flop," Franklin says. "Still, even though I go over headfirst and backward, it's not really the flop. When I take off, my take-off leg is stiff. Almost all the other jumpers have some give, or bend, in that leg.

"I think my technique works perfectly for me, but I wouldn't recommend it for anyone else. What I would tell young high jumpers is this: Use the style that's most natural and comfortable for you, the one that gets the best results. If you're good enough, a high-school or college coach will work on your technique later on."

What made Franklin Jacobs so special? He did something no other high jumper has come close to doing. While just a sophomore at Fairleigh Dickinson University, he set a world indoor record of 7'7¼". That means he jumped nearly two feet over his own height! "To be exact," Franklin says, "I was 5'8" at the time, so the jump was just three-quarters of an inch less than two feet. And I know I can go even higher. I want to do seven feet, ten inches before I finish jumping." That's what made Franklin special and what makes all the champions special.

7

Long Jumping

Good long jumpers are like good sprinters—and something more. Like sprinters, they have to be fast runners. Their muscles must be strong and have spring. They have to be able to lift their knees high. And they must be able to pace their runs, time themselves just right, and hit the take-off board at just the right moment, without the loss of speed and power. On top of all that, long jumpers have to be acrobatic. You'll see why later on.

There are four parts to a long jump: 1) the approach, 2) the take-off, 3) the sail, and 4) the landing. Let's look at them one by one, then put them all together.

The Approach. The best long jumpers dash down the runway from about 150 feet behind the take-off board. But a beginner is better off taking a shorter run, about 70 feet or so. (You can take increasingly longer approach runs after you have matured physically and have really learned the basic techniques of long jumping.) If your run is too long, you will be too tired to hit the take-off board with full strength. And if your run is too short, you won't have the speed needed to give your take-off height and distance.

Once you have decided where your best starting place is, practice sprinting down the runway to the take-off board.

After a few trial runs, decide which leg will be your take-off leg. Do this by running to the board and taking off on one leg. Then repeat the run so that you take off on the other leg. You'll soon be able to tell which leg gives you the stronger thrust up and away from the board.

Let's say you decided on the left leg. Okay, now go back to the starting line. You are ready to take your first really serious practice run. Toe the line with your left foot, and take the standing-start position.

Start running as fast as you can. When you have sprinted about 40 feet, remind yourself to keep your form and pace. Also concentrate your attention on the take-off board. (You might want to do what many long jumpers do: Put a marker on the ground right next to the 40-foot point. Then you'll know when you reach it, and how far you have to go.) Keep up the full sprint until you are two or three steps from the board. Then slow down just a little. You want to gather yourself for the spring into the air.

The Take-off. You want your take-off foot to hit the board solidly, right in the middle. Then the foot will go through a three-part action that should result in a perfect blast-off. The heel lands first, followed by the ball of the foot, then the toe.

Even as the heel-ball-toe action is taking place, the leg is bending at the knee. It bends just enough to spring you high and far into the air above the sandy pit.

Note: You should have stopped staring at the take-off board about five steps before reaching it. From then on, your head should be straight as you look at a point somewhere *beyond* the pit. This point is your target, the same way a sprinter's target is beyond the finish line.

As you begin to leap forward and up, tell yourself: The

*As you leap forward and up, snap the trailing leg forward,
stretch out those arms, and sail as far as you can.*

higher the better! At this moment, the trailing leg, which is coming up quickly, is bent at the knee. Straighten it as you begin to snap it forward.

Your right arm is swinging forward, your left arm is swinging backward. Your body is starting to rise into the air as your left foot leaves the board behind.

The Sail. This is the moment of lift-off! Your speed has made you a force hurtling through space. Your push-off foot must make you an even higher flying object by lifting you way up off the board.

You are airborne. Now, snap that take-off leg forward, to bring it up even with the front leg. You should then be sailing through the air as if you were sitting in a chair with both legs stretched in front of you.

While all this leg-and-body action is going on, your arms are working, too. Now, as you bring your legs together—stretching and pointing the toes toward the other end of the pit—reach forward with both hands until they are over your feet. This should put you into a jackknife position.

The Landing. You will, of course, try to sail as long as possible. But as gravity forces your body to come down, your arms will also begin to drop. Control their drop so that, before your heels hit the sand, you can swing both arms back as hard as possible. This will carry your body forward, which is what you want.

The distance of a long jump is measured from the point at which the jumper takes off to the mark nearest the board any part of the jumper's body makes in the pit. That's why you want to stay in the air as long as you can. And why you want your body to fall forward on landing.

There is a variation of long jumping called the hitch kick. It is the same as the jump just described, until the lift-off.

Control the drop of your arms so that, when your heels hit the sand, you can swing both arms back as hard as you can. This will carry your body forward for additional distance.

After lifting off, "run in the air." This means that, instead of bringing both your legs together, you continue the running motion you used when speeding to the take-off board.

The hitch kick style is so-called because you take three steps in midair after the takeoff. If you take off from the left foot, you will run right-left-right in the air. However, as you take that last step, your right leg will be coming even with your left leg. Both will be stretched out as far as possible, with your hands reaching out over your feet. Your landing actions will be the same as the ones for the first style of jump.

Training. Since long jumpers must be able to race down the runway like sprinters, they must follow the training of sprinters to a large extent. (See training schedule for sprinters.)

Long jumpers also must have good spring in their legs and the ability to sail through the air. Thus, workouts on a trampoline will do long jumpers a lot of good. Add to this the practice of tumbling like circus acrobats. This gives jumpers looseness of arms and legs and a better "feel" for bending and shifting in midair.

There is a special drill long jumpers use on the track or any other flat surface. While running along, leap into the air and keep on running, as if you are doing the hitch kick. After you land, run for five or six strides, then leap into the air again. Repeat this for 100 yards or so. The purpose of the drill is for you to practice getting off the ground as high as you can.

8

Triple Jumping

Many fans think the triple jump is the oddest and most difficult event in track and field. It certainly has a different look to it, and it definitely takes a really good athlete to do it right.

Triple jumpers use the same runway and landing pit as long jumpers do. In fact, the triple jump begins the same way, with the competitor sprinting down the runway. But it isn't long before the jumper meets the first difference between the long jump and the triple jump. For the triple jump, the take-off board is farther away from the landing pit. This is so to give the jumper the room needed to take a hop and a step before the jump. The hop, the step, the jump —those are the three parts of the triple jump.

Which foot should you use for the take-off from the board? Your stronger foot. Let's say your left foot is the stronger one. That means you will make the hop and the step with your left foot. The final move—the jump—will be done with your right foot.

The Hop. You are sprinting down the runway. Your body is low and bent slightly forward. You reach the take-off board. Your left foot slams down on the board. At the same time, your arms drive skyward in a strong thrust up and

Triple-jumpers sprint down the runway, gaining speed and power for the takeoff.

forward. As you take off, your body is just about straight up.

Your sail forward, *straight ahead*, chest straight and right knee raised. You *do not* want to move upward at the same time, as you would in the long jump.

The instant you feel yourself starting to come down, bring your arms down, too. Move them in a circular motion. That is because the next move will require you to thrust them up and forward again for the second part of the event, the step.

Land on your left foot. Keep your right leg bent at the level of your left knee. The right leg should be bent so that it is parallel to the ground.

The Step. Immediately after landing, you take off again on the same foot you landed on. As you push off the toes, use both arms for a powerful lift, the way you did on the hop. Also, keep your body straight, so you won't tilt too far forward or too far backward. And hold your lead leg up!

Note: One of the biggest difficulties triple jumpers have to overcome takes place during the step. This is caused by the natural desire of a jumper to reach for the ground with the lead leg. So, to combat this, remember to really push the knee of that lead leg up toward the chest.

As you begin to come down, bring your right foot forward and ready for its landing. Your body should be leaning slightly forward, getting into position for the final bounding leap of the triple jump!

The Jump. The right foot lands on its heel. A split second later, it has rocked quickly onto the ball, then the toes. Now it thrusts you forward and *up*.

This, the final phase of the triple jump, is like the take-off action of the long jump. You must force your body as high as it will go. Your momentum will carry your body toward

As you start to fall into the pit, get ready to land on your heels. Try to keep your feet in the air as long as you can. The longer you do, the farther you'll fly!

the landing area. At the same time, the trailing leg is coming up to be level with the leading leg. And your arms are reaching up.

At last, your body gets set for the landing. This also requires the same set of movements used in the long jump landing.

For a moment you were hanging in air on an invisible wire. Now you begin to swing your arms down. As you do, reach straight out with your hands. Your legs are stretched forward, bringing you into a sitting-in-air position. Hold this position as long as you can!

As gravity starts to push you back toward the pit, get ready to land on the heels of your feet. But don't drop your feet any sooner than you have to! The longer you stay airborne, flying forward, the better your distance will be.

Since this is a three-stage event, triple jumpers often practice the three separate stages individually. Then, when they feel ready, they put it all together, using the runway and the landing area.

The hop is practiced simply. Just run a short distance and hop. Run and hop. Run and hop. For variety, do some long hops, then switch off to some short, fast hops. Try for distance on some, then go for height on the next few hops.

Practice for the step is the same as the second part of this event. It's important to remember: 1) work to perfect the timing of the movements, and 2) lift the free leg high and keep the knee close to the chest.

Practicing the last part, the jump, is the same as practicing for the long jump. Special attention should be given to swinging the arms and legs forward to keep yourself in the air as long as possible.

Training. Training for the triple jump is the same as

Fall forward or sideways when you land. Distance is measured from the takeoff board to the point where any part of your body hits the sand.

training for the long jump. However, set aside some extra time for working on the hop and step portions of the event. It doesn't matter how well you can jump if you haven't put together the mechanics of a smooth hop and step.

One of America's best triple jumpers, Milan Tiff, said the event "is like playing hopscotch—only in a bigger way." To Tiff, a triple jump felt this way: "I'm coming down the runway, and I'm counting [my strides]. It takes me sixteen strides to get to the take-off board. As I hit the tenth stride, I say, 'Now, start propelling. Feel like you're a prop plane. When you hit the board, spin the propeller as hard as you can, and the motor will go *brrr*. And *boom!*, you're gone, just like a plane.'"

Tiff also likened the triple jump to a flat stone skimming over the water. "Watch it skip three or four times over the surface," he said. "There is something that hypnotizes you about that. Triple jump is the same thing, only you're hurling yourself through the air. You're actually flying!"

If you can feel that kind of excitement about the triple jump; if you can work and work at it until you have mastered all three parts and put them together into one smooth unit; if you can train and build your skills in the event . . . if you can do all those things, then maybe you, too, can "fly through the air" like a plane or a skipping stone.

9

Pole Vaulting

Pole vaulting is one of the most thrilling sights in sports. The athlete soars into the air, as high as 18 feet, and bends the body over a crossbar. This done, the vaulter completes the event by dropping straight down to a soft cushion of mats in the landing pit.

What does an athlete need to be able to fly like that? Courage, strength, coordination, and dedication to practice. Oh yes, he also needs a long pole.

Before any beginner starts to practice, the pole vaulter should make sure to do four things:

1. Warm up with stretches, calisthenics, and other exercises.

2. Check the equipment (pole, shoes, etc.).

3. Make sure the mats are in place in the landing pit.

4. Have at least one other person present (coach, parent, reliable friend).

These are all worthwhile safety measures. After all, it doesn't make sense to do things that will cause you to hurt yourself. And if, by accident, you do hurt yourself, it makes sense to have someone there to help you.

What qualities should a pole vaulter have? Being tall is an advantage, although a vaulter doesn't *have* to be tall.

The general run of vaulters is taller than average height. Vaulters should be in very good shape because the sport puts great demands on endurance and the strength of an athlete's arms, shoulders, back, and legs. Vaulters must also have enough speed of foot to give them the momentum to get up into the air, using the pole to balance and propel themselves. They also need a fine sense of timing and the physical ability to put together the different actions of the pole vault. And finally, they must not be afraid of the drop from the top of the vault to the landing pit far below.

A beginning vaulter should start to learn with a pole that tests about ten pounds more than he or she weighs. A clerk in a sporting goods store or a track coach can help you choose a pole that is the right weight and length for you.

Let's say you are right-handed. With that hand, grip the pole near its top end (where it is taped or has some other good gripping surface). The palm of that hand faces up. The left hand grips the pole a comfortable distance (two to three feet) ahead of the right hand. The left palm faces down.

Let's also say your right foot is the stronger foot. That's the foot you will take off from at the end of the run.

As you begin to move down the runway, the back of the pole should be carried about hip level, pointed straight ahead or slightly upward. (Some vaulters carry the pole higher than hip level. Find the grip and holding angle that suit you best. Once you do, try to practice that way consistently.) Your right arm is extended straight back and down. The left arm is bent at the elbow and held straight across the body at hip level.

The run down the runway usually begins slowly. You pick up speed as you get nearer the take-off point. Practice will give you the feeling for the pace of your approach. As an

As you move down the runway, carry the back of the pole at about hip level.

aid, however, you can put markers on the side of the runway. These will tell you when you have reached the places to increase your stride and/or your speed, and where to lower the pole in readiness for planting it in the vaulting box.

As you near the vaulting box, lower the tip of the pole. You are going to drive it straight into the box. Begin to dip the pole when you are about four strides from the box. The actual move to plant it takes place when you are two strides from the box. Don't forget: Keep the pole in a straight line! If you don't, it will tilt to one side or the other, and you will take off at an angle.

As you start to drop the tip of the pole, shift the positions of your hands. Swing the right hand forward and upward, so that it ends up in front of and above your head. The left hand slides until it is about 4-5 inches from the right hand. The left hand continues to guide the pole so that it points straight ahead and drives firmly into the box. Both arms are fully extended as the pole plant takes place.

Once the tip of the pole is set solidly against the back of the box, the muscles of your hands, arms, and shoulders come into play! Your tight grip on the pole must not be broken. The forward momentum will put mounting strain on your arm and shoulder muscles. This is where you will be rewarded for the hours of training that developed those muscles.

Now, as the pole begins to bend—it is becoming something like a slingshot or a catapult—you begin your takeoff. Your right leg—the stronger leg—pushes your body into the air, helping the pole do its job. Your left leg drives upward, bending at the knee, as if you are taking another stride. Keep in mind that, as the right leg finishes its push-off, the whole leg must be fully extended.

The instant your feet leave the ground, begin to swing your body upward and forward. You should be moving straight ahead and up, not off to one side. And, as you go up, bend your left arm at the elbow. This will keep your body from swinging past the pole as you climb higher.

The right arm also does its part in keeping control of the body. You bend it at the elbow, then "lock" your right shoulder. Now your body will not turn until you are ready to turn it. If you find, however, that you are turning in a slow spin during this part of the jump, it is probably because your arms are not in the right positions.

The pole has finished its bend. It will start to get straight. You will be reaching the peak of your upward swing. At that point, pull your body up. Your arm and shoulder muscles must do all the work. They will take over at the point where your own speed and the pole can't help anymore. But don't forget that the upward pull must be done at the exact instant just before your body reaches the peak of its swing.

The pole will be straight and only inches away from the crossbar. Don't worry. You are going to use it so that it will help you over the crossbar and then fall away when you are through with it.

Still gripping the pole with both hands, let your body begin to turn in a counterclockwise direction. When the turn is completed, you will be facing the runway. By this time your right leg will be almost even with your left leg. Both knees will be bent a little.

Now your body is both turning and continuing to rise. Your legs are almost together, and you are pushing hard on

The pole has finished its bend and is straight. The vaulter is almost at the peak of the upward swing.

the pole. A fraction of a section later, both legs will be above your head and—if you have done everything right—above the crossbar. You should be doing a midair handstand!

Let go of the pole with your left hand. Then, pushing up and away, your right hand also gets rid of the pole. The pole is about to go one way, and your body the other way, as it folds itself over the crossbar.

The last move is to snap your chest, head, and arms over the crossbar. Be especially careful not to let up and touch the bar with an arm or hand.

Finally, you can relax and let yourself fall into the soft cushion below. Take care not to land on your head or neck. The best place to land is on your back or side.

Training. It is not necessary to set a schedule, although you or your coach might want to. In any case, a variety of workouts should take place each week, with the following points in mind:

1) You should spend at least 30 minutes each day doing gymnastics, acrobatics, and/or working on a trampoline.

2) Spend at least two hours each week on running short sprints for speed and longer distances for endurance buildup. Proper use of weights for muscle development is also advisable.

3) Spend one hour each day on actual vaulting. Devote longer segments of time to those parts of the event that, for you, need the most work. *But be careful not to work out too long on vaulting.* Once you begin to feel tired or weak, stop! If you don't, you are asking to get hurt.

The following drills can be done just about anywhere:

1) Lift your left hand straight out from the shoulder. Kick at it with your right foot. Then, reverse, kicking your

Don't touch the bar with an arm or hand after the rest of you has cleared it.

This vaulter failed to clear the bar. But, he will relax and drop into the foam cushion below, landing on his back.

left foot at your right hand. Do five kicks on each foot, rest for a couple of minutes, then do ten more kicks.

2) Tie anything that weighs around five pounds to the ankle or foot of one leg. Now do the kick exercise described above. After ten kicks, tie the weight to the other foot or ankle, and do ten more kicks.

These drills will strengthen your leg muscles. Try to think of drills to strengthen your arm muscles for pole vaulting—drills that you can do anywhere. For example, anytime you are near a tree with branches two or three feet over your head, jump straight up, extending your arms all the way and reaching for the branch with your open hands. Then move away a few steps and lope toward the branch. Come to a stop just before you are under the branch and spring up, reaching for the branch with open hands. It takes a strong body and a strong mind to become a good pole vaulter. Are you ready to give it a really hard try? Good. And good luck!

THROWING EVENTS

10
Shot Putting

There is a very good reason for calling this event the shot put. The competitor must *put*—push or shove—the heavy metal ball. He or she must not try to throw the shot as if it were a baseball or football. A throwing motion can do great harm to the arm and shoulder muscles. So, when you put the shot, imagine that you are shoving something you hate, very much. That means you will shove it away with as much strength as you can get behind the up-and-out movement. But in order to get your weight and strength behind the shove, you have to learn and practice this field event very well.

An athlete below high-school age should work with a ball that weighs no more than eight pounds. In fact, it can weigh as little as four pounds. For boys of high-school age, twelve pounds is the advised top weight; the eight-pound shot is advised for girls. For college-age, male putters, the shot is a 16-pounder; for females, eight pounds, thirteen ounces.

The shot itself may be made of iron, steel, or brass. It is sometimes covered with rubber or leather for better gripping.

The circle from which the shot is put is seven feet across, and has a toe board at the front. The shot is thrown above the toe board. If you leave the circle any time during the put, you are charged with a foul and lose credit for that put.

The Hand Grip. The first thing you must learn is how to hold the shot. Let's assume you are right-handed. That means you will hold the shot in your right hand and use your right leg when you actually release the shot.

Set the metal ball onto your open hand, palm up. Rest it at the top of the palm (where the palm meets the finger). It should rest close to the thumb and index finger, because that is the strongest part of your hand. Now, spread your fingers until the shot sits comfortably and securely in your hand. Grip it firmly with all the fingers.

Next, tuck the shot against your neck, just under the right jawbone (about one inch under your right ear). Your right arm should be bent, the elbow pointing down and slightly away from your body.

Note: If the ball feels too heavy for your fingers, either get a lighter ball or practice with it resting on your palm until your fingers get stronger.

The Starting Position. Stand facing *away* from the toe board. Your feet will be near the back of the circle, the side opposite the toe board. Set your right foot near the back edge of the circle. Then move the left foot a few inches behind and to the left of the heel of the right foot.

Next, lean forward, shifting your weight over the right leg. Relax your shoulders, and tilt your head just a bit forward. Lift your left arm up and out, to aid your balance. Once you are set, lift your left leg until it is bent at the knee and the foot is pointing at the ground. Look straight ahead. Do not try to look over your shoulder in the direction you will be throwing.

The Drive. Bend forward from the waist, bringing your

With the shot against your neck, lean forward, using your left arm for balance. Lift the left leg until it is bent at the knee and the foot is pointing toward the ground.

body over your right leg. Then powerfully kick your left leg back toward the toe board. At the same time, push off with your right leg. You should push so hard with the right leg that you take a short backward hop toward the toe board.

Next, bring your left foot down, just behind the toe board, and pull your right leg close in and under your body. You are still facing away from the toe board. Your drive has taken you well past the middle of the circle. Your body weight is still over your right leg, but is beginning to shift. Your left arm is raised, balancing the body. Your hips and shoulders are starting to turn to the left toward the toe board.

The Turn and the Put. Now, *lift* from your right leg and hip. At the same time, swing your left arm around and up. Finish the turn, bringing your left foot hard against the toe board. While you are smoothly going through these movements, you are gripping the shot—shooting the right arm up and forward—and shoving that metal ball high and far away from you!

The power behind the put comes from 1) the left leg kicking back hard, 2) the momentum built by the turn, 3) the right leg driving the body up, which 4) carries the force through the right hip, on up into the right shoulder and, finally, 5) into the hand gripping the metal ball.

Finishing Up. Even as the ball is leaving your hand, you are shifting your feet for the follow-through. This foot-shifting action is intended to stop your forward movement. Remember: You must not leave the circle until the put is complete!

Simply said, what you have to do to stop is lift your left foot from the ground and instantly replace it with your right foot. And, at the moment your right foot touches the

As you release the shot, keep your form in the follow-through. Remember to push up through the right hip, into the right shoulder, and into the hand holding the ball.

ground, twist it so that its right side is pressed against the toe board.

As the shot begins to arc through the air, this is the position you should be in: You are standing on your right foot. Your left leg is extended behind you, the foot raised off the ground. Your right arm, following through on the put, is beginning to reach waist level. Your left arm is extended out to the left, like a bird's wing. Your eyes are following the flight of the shot, so your head is lifted.

Training Schedule

Monday: Warm up for five minutes—stretching, toe-touching, etc. Take three practice puts. Decide on which part needs the most work and give 15 minutes to that.

Do two 50-yard sprints. Complete a circuit of the track at an easy run.

Do three more puts. Concentrate on technique, not the distance of the put.

Do a medium-fast, quarter-mile run.

Tuesday: Warm-up exercises for five minutes. Work on each part of the event: the start, the drive, the turn and put, the finish. Then do a 30-minute workout, with most of the time spent on correcting weaknesses.

Do a medium-fast, quarter-mile run, followed by two 50-yard sprints. Take a ten-minute rest.

Work on weights, following your coach's suggestions.

Wednesday: Warm up.

Work only on trying to eliminate weaknesses, for 30 minutes.

As you release the shot, don't forget to give it that extra clock-wise twist for extra distance.

Do three puts without using the shot.
Make three competitive puts.
Do a quarter-mile jog, followed by a 100-yard sprint.

Thursday: Warm up.
Make three competitive puts.
Spend 15 minutes on trying to correct weaknesses.
Work on weights.

Friday: If there is a meet the next day, just do warm-up exercises and run easy laps around the track. If there is no meet scheduled, follow Thursday's program.

11
Discus Throwing

Like the shot putter, the discus thrower must not leave the throwing circle until the throw is done. And, like the shot putter, a discus thrower has to be strong and ready to work hard at developing the techniques of the event.

The discus is held in your stronger hand. (Let's assume your right hand is the stronger one.) Most discus throwers use one of two grips:

1) The talon or claw grip, with all the fingers spread over the edge of the discus. The fingertips hold the discus so that they look like the talons of an eagle holding onto a branch.

2) The index and middle finger held together, with the other fingers spread.

In both styles, the palm of the hand is pressed against the middle of the discus.

Whichever grip you use, hold the edge of the discus against the joints of the fingers (but not the thumb) closest to your fingernails. The middle finger is the strongest and carries most of the force of the throw. Even so, the platelike discus must be thrown so that it rolls off the fingers—index finger first, little finger last.

There are four basic steps in throwing the discus: 1) the swinging start, 2) the turn, 3) the throw, and 4) the finish.

The Swinging Start. Take your starting position at the

back of the circle. Point your feet slightly to the left and right, making a V. Hold the discus in your right hand, palm down, and balance it underneath with your left hand, palm up. Bend your knees a bit.

Now, raising the discus to shoulder level, extend your hands in front of you. The right elbow is slightly bent. The left elbow is bent much more because the balancing hand is below the discus. As soon as you are set, start to swing the discus to the left side. Your left hand lets go of the discus and becomes a balance for the left side of your body.

When you have swung as far to the left as you can, swing the discus across your body to the right as far as you can. After two or three left-right swings, you are ready to start the turn.

The swings do three things: 1) get the muscles loose and moving, 2) get you into the rhythm and timing of the event, and 3) get your momentum started for the coming turn motion.

While your arms are swinging, your body is also swinging gently at the hips in the same direction as the discus. And your weight is shifting from one foot to the other. Thus, when your weight is on your right foot, the discus will be swung over to the right side. And when your weight is on your left foot, the discus will be swung over to the left side. As the right hand swings the discus out, the left hand and arm are extended from the shoulder to the left for balance.

The Turn. Your right arm has just carried the discus out to the right. Now, you are going to do one-and-a-half spins. First, your left leg bends, the knee goes about halfway to the ground and starts to turn to the left. As the body spins to the left, the right leg swings out and around. At this point the discus is well behind your back.

Next, push off from your left foot and bring your right

94

The opening, left-to-right swings get the muscles loose and moving for the turn that follows.

As you complete the turn, bring the left foot down, drop the left arm, and bring the discus across your body at a slight upward angle.

foot down in the center of the ring. As the right foot lands, the left foot is coming up. Your left arm is still out for balance, your shoulders are squared, and the discus is behind your back.

Thus far, the turn has been done at half-speed. Now, quickness is required for the rest of the throw.

Continue to turn on your right foot, and bring your body around toward the front of the circle. Then, bring your left foot down near the front edge of the circle. At the same time, lower your left arm and bring your right arm across your body at a *slight* upward angle. (Throwing the discus high is not the way to get good distance on a throw.) The hand holding the discus should come from as far in back of the body as possible.

The Throw. At the instant your left foot hits the ground, it will bring you to a sudden stop. This will give a slingshot effect to your throw, since the rest of your body will still be spinning. Here is where the explosive throw takes place. The right hip whips around in the direction of the throw. The chest, shoulder and arm muscles send their power into the throw. And the index and middle fingers snap the discus away when it is about head high, giving it a whirling motion that helps it to sail on the wind. (Anyone who understands what makes a Frisbee fly far will understand the theory of throwing a discus, as well as the technique.)

The Finish. Once the discus is flying away, the right arm will follow through by swinging beyond the edge of the circle. Then it will continue across the left side of the body, and down. Finally, as in the shot put, the right foot will come down close to the left foot. And, as it does, you will lift your left foot off the ground. At this point, some discus throwers continue to spin around on the right foot. It is their

The perfect form for the throw is shown by Al Oerter, winner of four consecutive Olympic gold medals in the discus event. His right hip is whipping around in the direction of the throw; his

chest, arm, and shoulder muscles sending a huge rush of power into the release of the disc. The index and middle fingers will give it a whirling motion as it sails up and away.

As the discus is released, the right arm follows through. It swings past the circle, then across the left side of the body, and down.

way of controlling the momentum caused by the increase in the body speed on the last turn.

Training schedule

Monday, Tuesday, Wednesday: Warm up for five minutes by jogging easily, doing stretch exercises, and/or calisthenics.

Do three throws without a discus.

Do three throws with a discus, but not for distance. Stress timing and rhythm, and smoothness of the four-step procedure.

Work to correct weaknesses for five minutes each.

Do two throws, again for timing, rhythm, and smoothness.

Do ten minutes of throwing for distance. Work on snap-release and angle at the moment of release (about 30° above the horizontal).

Do an easy jog around the track.
Work on weights. Follow coach's instructions regarding heaviness of weights, time given to workouts, and so forth.

Thursday: Warm up for five minutes.

Do two throws without a discus, two with a discus.

Work for five minutes on each step of the four-step procedure.

Work for ten minutes to eliminate weaknesses.

Jog around the track. Do several short wind sprints.
Do a light weight workout.

Friday: If competing on Saturday, just warm up, do five throws without a discus, then jog around track. If there is no meet on Saturday, repeat Thursday's schedule.

12

Javelin Throwing

Another field event that calls for speed, strength, and timing is the javelin throw. The javelin, or spear, is about 8½ feet long and weighs about two pounds. It has three parts: the tail, the tip, and the grip, or cord. You hold the javelin in the grip area. The body is made of wood or light metal, the tip of a hard metal. Always throw the javelin tip-first. If it lands on its tail, the javelin can be ruined.

The javelin is held at an angle in the palm of your stronger hand. (Let's say your right hand is the stronger one.) The javelin will lie between the thumb and the index finger, slightly nearer the index finger. The middle finger, ring finger, and little finger hold the cord, with the middle finger gripping it the most. The index finger either rests on the shaft or curls around it. The javelin is held in this position, palm up, from start to finish. Remember, however, to hold the javelin with just enough force to control it. Do not squeeze it tightly.

The javelin throw consists of four stages or steps: 1) the approach, 2) the setup for the throw, 3) the throw, and 4) the follow-through or finish.

The Approach. The approach takes place on the runway, which is 120 feet long. The first part of the approach is done

The approach begins with the javelin held above the shoulder, the tip pointed at the target area.

by running at a *controlled* speed. (Beginners should start with a slow run, increasing speed only when technique and timing are good.)

As you start to make this run, carry the javelin above your right shoulder and a bit above head level. The tip is pointed at the target area. (The javelin should be thrown right down the middle of the target area. As your run takes you closer to the throwing line, carry the javelin farther behind you, the tip tilted higher and higher. The first part of the approach will take seven or nine strides. (Don't forget: right-handed throwers should start on the left foot and finish on the left foot.)

The second part of the approach begins after your seventh (or ninth) stride. This is when you start to move the javelin forward and tilt it upward. Now you have five more strides to get into a javelin-launching position.

The first stride will be off your left foot and onto your right foot. The right foot should be pointing out (to the right) at a 45-degree angle when it lands. As this is taking place, your arm is bringing the javelin back.

The second stride will bring your left foot to the ground. It will land so that it is pointing a little to the *right*. Meanwhile you have moved the javelin farther back, the tip pointing a bit higher.

The Setup for the Throw. On the third stride, turn your body to the right. This means that, when the right foot lands, your chest will be almost at a right angle to the direction in which you are running.

Your left arm should be raised and bent slightly at the elbow. It should point in the same direction as your right foot. You have by now dipped the javelin farther back, the tip pointing higher.

Getting ready to launch the javelin, the thrower's body is turned to the right. When the right foot lands, the chest will be almost at a right angle to the target area.

This stride is part of the two-part cross-step. The left foot will come down and "plant" itself, hitting heel-first. The right foot will cross over the left foot as it takes stride four.

While your feet are doing the cross-step, your left arm (which has been held out as an aid to balance) starts to swing around to the left. Your weight is coming down fully on your left leg. Your head is turned a little to the left (but not so much that you lose sight of the throwing line). This will help you to guide the javelin through on a straight line.

The Throw. On the next step, number five, you thrust the javelin forward and up. It is now pointed at a 30-to-40-degree angle. Your left arm is swinging down, as your whole body sends power surging into the javelin. This power comes from the momentum of your approach, and the push that starts in your feet and legs, back and shoulders—and *pours* into your right arm.

All of this is completed by the whipping motion of your hand as it sends the javelin flying up and away. The throw is like pulling on a chain, behind you, as if you are trying to pull it away from an anchor.

The Follow-through or Finish. The finish must be done correctly, or your feet could go past the foul line. This means that, after your throw off the left foot, you must bring the right leg forward quickly. Then, finally, land on it with your body well balanced.

Training Schedule

Monday: Do light calisthenics. Spend at least one hour on some activity to strengthen the body, such as running, swimming, or gymnastics.

The two-part cross-step. The left foot comes down and "plants" itself, hitting heel-first. Then the right foot crosses over the left foot.

On the throw, the left arm swings down, and the power of the whole body is sent into the javelin. Finally, the javelin is set in flight by a thrust of the arm and a whipping motion of the hand.

Tuesday: Do a five-minute warm-up. Take one lap around the track at an easy pace.

Do three throws, without the javelin.

Practice the cross-step for 15 minutes. It is the most important part of the event for beginners to learn correctly.

Do three throws, with the javelin, but do not concentrate on distance. Instead, work on technique and timing.

Work on correcting weaknesses.

Wednesday: Do one lap around the track at an easy pace.

Do five throws, without the javelin.

Do three throws, with the javelin, at three-quarters strength.

Work on eliminating weaknesses.

Thursday: Repeat Wednesday's schedule, plus light weight workout. As always, consult your coach regarding use of weights.

Friday: If there is a meet on Saturday, do light calisthenics and practice five throws, without the javelin. If there is no meet, follow Tuesday's schedule.

Index

Index

Approach, in long jump, 59-60

Bannister, Roger, 31
Baton passing, 15-19
    passing zone, 16, 19

Claw grip, in the discus, 93
Closed baton pass, 16, 19

Dashes, 3, 5-9
Decathlon, x
Discus throwing, 93-101
    finish, 97-100
    swinging start, 93-94
    throw, 97
    training for, 101
    turn, 94-97
Distance races, 31-41
Drive, in the shot put, 86-88

880-yard run, xi, 32-34
Exercises (warming up), 43-48

Fairleigh Dickinson
    University, 57

1500-meter run, xi, 32, 34-36
50-meter dash, 3
50-yard dash, 3
50-yard hurdles, 26
Finishes, 3, 9-10
Flop, in the high jump, 51,
    54-57
4 x 110-yard relay, 15
4 x 440-yard relay, 15
4 x 220-yard intermediate
    hurdles, 22
440-yard run, 3, 10-12
400-meter intermediate
    hurdles, 22
400-meter run, 3, 10-11

Handgrip, in shot put, 86
High jumping, 51-57
Hop, in the triple jump, 65-67
Hop, step and jump (see triple
    jumping)
Hurdles, high, 22
Hurdles, low, 22
Hurdling, 21-30
Hurdling, training for, 28-30

Jacobs, Franklin, 57
Javelin throwing, 103-110
    approach, 103-105
    controlled speed, 105
    finish, 107
    setup, 105-107
    throw, 107
    training for, 107-110
Jump, in the triple jump, 67-69

Landing, in the long jump,
  62-64
Leonard, Silvio, 10
Long-distance running, 36-41
Long jump, training for, 64
Long jumping, 59-64
    hitch kick, 62, 64

Marathon, ix, 31, 36-41
Mile run, 32, 34-36

Nehemiah, Renaldo, 26-28

Olympics, 1972, 31
180-yard low hurdles, 22
100-meter dash, 8-11
1000-yard run, 32-34
110-meter high hurdles, 22, 26
120-yard high hurdles, 22
100-yard dash, xi, 8-11
Open baton pass, 16

Pole vaulting, 73-82
    safety measures, 73
    training for, 79-82

Relays, 15-19

Rodgers, Bill, 41
Ryun, Jim, 31

Sail, in the long jump, 62
Shorter, Frank, 31, 38-41
Shot putting, 85-92
    starting position, 86
    training for, 90-92
    weights of, 85
Sprint medley relay, 15-16
Sprinting, 3-13
Sprints, training for, 12-13
Starting blocks, 3-8
Starts, 3
Step, in the triple jump, 67
Straddle, in the high jump,
  51-54

Take-off, in the long jump,
  60-62
Talon grip, in the discus, 93
Tiff, Milan, 71
Triple jumping, 65-71
    training for, 69-71
Trampoline, 64, 79
Turn and put, in the shot
  put, 88
200-meter sprint, 8, 10
220-yard sprint, 10-11

Viren, Lasse, 31

Warming up, 43-48
Weight training, 13
Williams, Steve, 8, 10-12
World's Fastest Human, x
World's Greatest Athlete, x

DATE			
NOV 16	MR 19 '85		
DEC 2	AP 25 '86		
FEB 15			
APR 21	NO -7 '86		
JU 08 87	NOV 9 1987		
OC 19			
NO 16	DEC 5 1988		
NO 30 83	FACULTY		
DE 05 83			
AP 04 '84	APR 5 1989		
MY 23 84	MAY 10 1990		
OC 24 84			